Knitting With Barbed Wire

Knitting With Barbed Wire

UNDERSTANDING THE FACTOR OF RELIGION
IN MENTAL ILLNESS AND HEALTH

❖

Marcia A. Murphy

RESOURCE *Publications* · Eugene, Oregon

KNITTING WITH BARBED WIRE
Understanding the Factor of Religion in Mental Illness and Health

Copyright © 2024 Marcia A. Murphy. All rights reserved. Except for brief quotations in critical publications or reviews, no part of this book may be reproduced in any manner without prior written permission from the publisher. Write: Permissions, Wipf and Stock Publishers, 199 W. 8th Ave., Suite 3, Eugene, OR 97401.

Resource Publications
An Imprint of Wipf and Stock Publishers
199 W. 8th Ave., Suite 3
Eugene, OR 97401

www.wipfandstock.com

PAPERBACK ISBN: 979-8-3852-2381-7
HARDCOVER ISBN: 979-8-3852-2382-4
EBOOK ISBN: 979-8-3852-2383-1

Scripture quotations marked (ESV) are from The Holy Bible, English Standard Version (ESV), copyright ©2001 by Crossway Bibles, a publishing ministry of Good News Publishers. Used by permission. All rights reserved.

Scripture quotations marked (NIV) are taken from the Holy Bible, New International Version®, NIV®. Copyright © 1973, 1978, 1984, 2011 by Biblica, Inc.™ Used by permission of Zondervan. All rights reserved worldwide. www.zondervan.com The "NIV" and "New International Version" are trademarks registered in the United States Patent and Trademark Office by Biblica, Inc.™

*This is dedicated to all the misfits and outcasts,
people on the margins*

The pen is mightier than the sword.
—EDWARD BULWER-LYTTON,
BRITISH NOVELIST, AND PLAYWRIGHT

Contents

Author's Note viii

Chapter 1 Two Sisters 1

Chapter 2 Psych Unit 8

Chapter 3 Knitting With Barbed Wire 17

Chapter 4 No Place to Call Home 33

Chapter 5 Importance of God for Mental Health 39

Conclusion 53

Bibliography 57

Author's Note

THIS IS A WORK of creative nonfiction. In order to protect the privacy of individuals involved some names, characteristics, and locations have been altered. The exceptions are names of prominent figures and institutions which are known to the public.

1

Two Sisters

ONCE UPON A TIME there was a beautiful girl. She was the most beautiful girl in the entire world. Nobody on earth was as beautiful as she was. She was so beautiful that every time she looked at herself in the mirror (which was quite frequently), the mirror shined brightly with golden light radiating outward, filling the entire room.

When the beautiful girl was young she spent almost all of her free time doing physical exercise so she could tone her muscles and lose weight. The only food she would usually eat was chilled, raw vegetables, canned fruit with cottage cheese, and microwaved snack-sized Jimmy Dean sausage biscuits with diet pop. Her fenced in backyard was perfect for spreading out her brightly colored beach towel during the hot summer days when she could sunbathe in her two-piece bikini while spraying baby oil on her tender white skin and hydrogen peroxide in her hair. By fall, she emerged a bronzed-baked and blond-streaked doll.

The beautiful girl's father was an oil tycoon who made it rich in the grand state of Texas, but when she was three years old her parents got divorced. During the beautiful girl's teenage years, her mother, a nonstop talker (about nothing of value), took her on vacation trips to Las Vegas where they saw lots of shows and gambled. They also went on shopping trips to Neiman Marcus and other stores in downtown Dallas. Once or twice a year they'd fly out to California to shop on Rodeo Drive in Beverly Hills. Back in Texas her mother gave her driving lessons in their purple Panamera GTS Porsche.

The beautiful girl had one other sibling, a twin sister, who was adopted out shortly after birth because the parents wanted nothing to do with her because she had a large, dark brown birthmark on the inside of her ankle—which they considered to be an ugly and permanent blemish. When the beautiful girl reached seventeen years of age, she decided to skip college and try her luck in the modeling industry since she knew she was incredibly beautiful. All the high school boys had fought to get a chance to take her out on a date but only a few succeeded. Graphic and boisterous were the many tales of their exploits in the school locker room.

The beautiful girl was lonely. Her family was not part of a religious congregation where she could have met friends so when she reached the legal age, she spent time sitting in bars striking up conversations with strangers. The beautiful girl, now a young woman, wanted to apply at modeling agencies; that's how she and her mother ended up living in the sunny state of California. They found a place to live which happened to be only a few blocks down from a upper-middle class Christian church. During rare moments of introspection, the beautiful young woman wondered about God, if a god existed, and so she felt drawn to the church. Out of curiosity, she decided to try attending a worship service. On the morning of the service the girl entered the building and she noticed a bold, colorful poster on the wall beckoning all to join the Women's Knitting Group. They met on Monday evenings at seven o'clock on the lower level. It said all are welcome to be there.

The worship service was full of inspiring (though a bit loud) music and, afterwards, during fellowship time, she approached the cookies and coffee set on a table in the hope of striking up conversation but the whole crowd would, as one, move down away from her. She found this astonishing. She thought how she had found the pastor's sermon interesting because it was about the woman at the well with Jesus. The woman at the well came there at noon to avoid the usual group of women who usually came there early in the morning. She felt inferior and feared gossip and mistreatment from the group. But Jesus welcomed her there and spoke kindly to her, engaging her in nonjudgemental conversation. When the beautiful girl approached the pastor to thank him for the good sermon the pastor reached out to shake her hand. However, he held her hand a little too long and a little too tightly, then winked at her.

She never went back.

As the young woman got started in her modeling career she came under the control of an older, dark, sinister man she met in a North Hollywood single's bar who wanted her to sell herself for money. He threatened to kill her mother if she refused to obey him. She was caught in the pimp's clutches and felt no alternative but to submit. Eventually, however, her mother, (who was a chain-smoker to help maintain her weight) died from lung cancer, so the pimp could no longer use his threat.

The young woman felt trapped. She had become the pimp's ring leader in his harem of prostitutes and she was told to groom the other girls for the sex trade. The pimp was abusive and there was a lot of physical, emotional, and sexual abuse. It got to be too much, she even suffered a broken collar bone. Then she got pregnant and had also contracted lots of STDs and she could not find any place to receive medical care. All the clinics rejected her because she lacked insurance or cash.

One night, the young woman planned her escape and then the next morning just before sunrise, ran away. She left her baby behind because she had no way to take care of the baby on the run. She was free at last, but she didn't have any money and was sleeping on the streets. Eventually, a homeless man took her in but only to his tent on the sidewalk of Skid Row. During daylight hours she panhandled to try to get enough cash for food. One day a squeaky-clean, blond, shaven, young man wearing a Salvation Army cap handed her a tract between her bouts of vomiting as she sat on the curb. On the tract was scripture from the Bible, the book of John, chapter fourteen. She needed eye glasses and could not make out the text; and she felt so sick she couldn't even try to read it. She just crumpled up tract and threw it down into the muddy gutter. The young man knelt down on one knee and tried to engage the young woman in conversation. He invited her to the Corps' building for a meal and prayer group meeting after a sermon preached by their pastor.

Nauseous, the young woman shook her head and told him, "No."

He got up, patted her on the shoulder, and walked away.

By now, the young woman's health had deteriorated to such an extent that she became gravely ill. Her weight dropped so much she was only skin and bones. The untreated STDs ravaged her body and infected her brain, driving her insane. The young woman found a drug dealer and persuaded him to give her some fentanyl in exchange for a few tricks which she overdosed on . . . and died from. For a while, nobody saw her barely clad dead body in the alley. Rats nibbled on her corpse while cockroaches crawled all over her face and into her ears. Finally, a large garbage truck rolled through the alley on its route. The truck's muscular workers picked up and threw the girl's body into the bowels of the crusher where she perished. No one ever knew what became of her.

*

The young woman stirred in her bed and suddenly bolted upright, letting out a terrible scream, awakening from the horrific nightmare. On the back of one hand, a large IV needle was stuck in a vein causing excruciating pain. A clear liquid flowed down from a thin tube connected to a bottle which hung from a pole at the side of her bed. On another side a machine with lights blinked at her, occasionally beeping. She was surprised to find that her recently polished inches-long, manicured fingernails had been trimmed to the quick. Strands of her now shorn bleached-blond hair were sticking out in all directions she felt with her free hand. Her gray hospital gown was loosely fitting with a bedsheet pulled up just under her chest. Her dirty bare feet were exposed and her toes felt cold.

What am I doing here? She wondered.

Just then, a middle-aged East Indian doctor in a long, white lab coat walked in, a stethoscope dangling from around his neck.

"How are you doing, Ms.? That was quite a fall last night. Luckily, our boys got to you in time. How does your head feel? Now, why don't you tell me why you wanted to do such a drastic thing, taking that drug—jumping from the car ramp. You must have known it wasn't high enough, just the second floor. Luckily, no bones are broken except for your right ankle—which is pretty severe—so we'll have to put a cast on it instead of using a medical boot. After we do that, you'll be transferred to the psychiatric unit."

The woman couldn't answer the doctor's question because a sedative given to her earlier rendered her speechless. The physician proceeded to check some vitals, the bump on her forehead, and swollen ankle. Then he gave some orders to a short, plump, red-headed RN who had just entered the room. The young woman suddenly felt famished and asked for some food. The nurse explained how she could order it on a phone that was on the bedside table. The young woman managed to do that herself. She felt grateful that the suicide attempt had been a failure. At least now she could think of better ways to live her life; but she'd need help in doing that. She felt she needed lots of therapy, someone who would listen with compassion, and who could advise her.

*

Meanwhile, unbeknownst to the beautiful young woman, her twin sister miles away out in the Midwest, walked across an auditorium stage to receive her diploma at Good Intentions University. She wore a long, immaculate, black, flowing gown with her thick, shoulder-length, brunette hair pulled up in a French twist. Her necklace held a slender wooden cross, emblematic of her Savior. Though also a beauty, she was one who wore wire-rim spectacles, no make-up, and natural hair color. She chose to develop her talents with reading, possessing the gift of studiousness while in school. She didn't date because no one asked her out: all of the young college men were too intimidated by her intellect, avoiding, even shunning her. At parties, they would talk behind her back and make fun of her, some of which she overheard. Now, after obtaining her Bachelor's degree, she would continue on into Graduate school to work on a Masters and PhD with a primary focus on the philosophy of religion. She also wanted to be a writer, not necessarily a famous or best-selling author, but one who wrote about worthwhile topics and justice issues that with good marketing, could possibly initiate changes in society.

This sister had lost touch with her biological family since the time she was born, and instead, she emotionally bonded with, first, her foster parents, and then a few months later, with a permanent set of the adoption parents who legally gave her their surname. In the adopted family the parents valued missionary work, they had spent time in Sub-Saharan Africa as a pastor and teacher. They instilled in the girl a love for scripture and Sunday worship. Back in the states on sabbaticals, they regularly attended services and events at a traditional Lutheran religious community where the Sunday School lessons for the children had an influence of producing good character development and would instill wholesome values. She learned how to see herself in a healthy way, and to also show respect toward other people.

This sister's parents and church taught that human sexuality was God's gift in a committed relationship. She learned that material possessions were also God's gift to help us with our daily lives, not to be hoarded or gluttonously, craved. Money was something to help us acquire practical things for our day-to-day survival. Greed was a sin. Not helping others with our resources, sharing with those less fortunate, was also a sin punishable by God.

This sister learned that her own personal physical beauty reflected God's beauty and was not something to be idolized in self-worship. Vanity or vainglory, was the sin of egotistical pride which God also punishes. But even though she knew that God punishes, she also knew he does so reluctantly. She knew that God hates our suffering even more than we do ourselves. It was precisely this problem of human suffering that led this sister to become a hospital chaplain. Her studies in the religion field were more than adequate background; and her hands-on training brought her to the western United States and there she visited patients on a psychiatric unit.

2

Psych Unit

THE CHAPLAIN SISTER LOVED her new work but found it challenging. There were so many patients and so very little time. Each day she had to scurry from one place to another, one room, then the next. And the patients were very sick, incredibly ill. Outside the hospital not many had enough resources to survive on their own and with lack of food, adequate clothing, and shelter they often become homeless, starving, and suffered from heat/cold exposure. Many turned to alcohol or illicit drug use to try to escape their misery. Many, abandoned by family and friends, had nowhere to turn. Some walked into the ER asking for help; others were arrested for trespassing or picked up in other ways.

The emergency department was overflowing with desperate people and this alarmed the hospital administration who sought ways to keep up. Budgets were tight and the high turnover of burned-out staff left the wards crippled. Things were in every aspect an on-going crisis situation. This is what the chaplain encountered during her first year of training with the psych unit. Alarmingly, she heard that sometimes in other parts of the nation, hospital security staff would in the middle of the night escort some of the psych patients out the door and over to Greyhound bus terminals where they were sent with a one-way ticket to a far-off state.

How could her spiritual counseling be of any use? She wondered. *First, just give them hope. Having hope is the foundation of change and a vision for the future*, she thought. *Without hope, nothing else matters. Hope is a frame of mind and a habit of thought that can guide our way out of darkness and despair.*

One patient named Sue, had been seriously considering assisted suicide. Her relatives convinced her to check in to the psych unit so she could think things over with the aid of the mental health professionals. It seemed to her that death was the logical choice because she had dealt with clinical depression for as long as she could remember and her condition never improved. Now, at the age of thirty-one, her distress was so acute that she was ready to throw in the towel. The hospital offered her transcranial magnetic stimulation (TMS); however, during the procedure, a seizure occurred which stopped the process and they discontinued it. Also, she felt that it was just the situation where she was given caring attention by the healthcare staff that boosted her mood and comforted her since she lived alone in isolation; not the electric brain treatment. Being at the hospital gave her somewhere to go to be around people and she enjoyed eating at the hospital cafeteria. So it wasn't the electronic therapy that helped, it was all the other things surrounding the event that contributed to her improved mood. But once she returned to her apartment, the same depression returned. She would sit in her living room chair and stare out the window. On a good day Sue could read a little, mostly short novels, but once in a while some longer Russian works. She had tried religion, had gone to a church for a worship service, but nobody there would talk to her, so she just quickly left, embarrassed.

Sue had a lot in common with Mary, another suicidal patient, who suffered from chronic physical pain and who had not found relief. Mary had sought a diagnosis from many doctors but they mostly gaslit her and blew off her concerns because she was bipolar. The doctors figured it was all a figment of her imagination and they didn't want to follow up with tests or medical treatments. Mary's pain was excruciating on a daily basis, affected both of her lower limbs. She went in a period of seven years from walking with a cane, to one crutch, to two forearm crutches, to a wheelchair. Mostly, now, she used forearm crutches and a wheelchair, and was dependent on those for support. Mary spent a great deal of time fantasizing about ways to kill herself because the pain was unbearable. She went on-line and Googled Benadryl to see how much it cost and what form it came in, whether in liquid form or tablets. She found stores that sold it, a Walgreens nearby had it in stock.

When Sue and Mary came across each other on the psych unit it was as though they had been soulmates for a lifetime. At first, rather shy and withdrawn, they both finally emerged from their emotional cocoons and began conversing though rather tentatively. Their interests in researching suicidal methods was a main topic. They mostly sat together mornings on the unit's outdoor patio in the back that was shaded by trees. The fenced-in courtyard was a reprieve from the chaotic environment of the busy and crowded indoor hospital unit. It was there that the chaplain approached the young women and invited them both to a patient support group meeting. Sue and Mary turned and looked at each other, then they both answered the chaplain in the affirmative.

Now, the chaplain also asked the beautiful young woman to participate in the support group, but the young woman said: "No, not interested!" She mainly sat alone in a corner of the Day Room watching TV or would strike up conversations with the other patients, those who also looked drugged out. She particularly approached the ones with tattoos and dyed hair of bizarre colors and weird styles. Her main interest now was food and she ate heartily at mealtimes along when the snack cart came out three times a day. She gained so much weight that the nursing staff had to find her large-sized sweatpants in storage to help her feel more comfortable. Sweatpants were donated on a regular basis by a local religious organization which the staff greatly appreciated.

Promptly, at two o'clock, the group session began in a large room with drab décor. There were nine patients, both male and female sitting in a circle along with the chaplain who started with a general inquiry: "Who would like to open with an answer to the question: "What brought you here to the hospital, the psych unit specifically?"

Mary, the one with lower limb pain, blurted out uncharacteristically: "I've tried everything to relieve my pain. The Wahls Protocol Diet was too expensive so I couldn't go on that! It's only for the wealthy! I tried swimming laps and walking in water at the city pool but that only made things worse. I could barely make it home on foot after a workout and the pain increased for several days as though I had damaged the muscles. I was confined to a wheelchair. For years I've tried everything: soaking in a hot bath; staying immobile and resting for periods of time to see it that would help. But for the past seven years the discomfort has increased to the point of my mind being obsessed with it. Since I have a bipolar diagnosis, the neurologists are prejudiced and won't provide follow-up or long-term treatment, they don't think I'm worth it. It's discrimination, that's what it is! I'm just a dumb mental patient with delusions! Not worth their time!"

The chaplain took notes on a scratch pad looking up often to make eye contact with the patient doing the speaking. Next, Bev jumped in and expressed similar frustrations of not finding any relief from her depressed mood which was worsened when all the medical attempts to cure her had failed.

"I've tried CBT (Cognitive Behavior Therapy), antidepressants, individual psychotherapy, electronic brain stimulation techniques—but nothing works. My relatives are not supportive; they are so dysfunctional that any thought of them makes me feel nauseous."

Just then Jeremy spoke up. Normally a quiet, bookish sort, he couldn't help himself when all the complaints left out one important component.

"Where is God in all this? Has anyone dared to ask?"

The room was suddenly still and profoundly quiet, all eyes on Jeremy. He continued.

"It appears to me that we have left out the factor of faith. Has anyone prayed for healing? Or if not healing, for some kind of answers to our dilemmas?"

The chaplain straightened in her chair and thought, *This is my cue*. She cleared her throat and began.

"Spirituality can often be a helpful thing when we are ill, either physically, emotionally, or both. Has anyone ever found the concept of a god useful?"

The room was silent. Just Jeremy raised his hand in acknowledgment and dropped it again. The chaplain continued.

"I believe that humans are made up of body, mind, and spirit, and often times when we pray this can help relieve some of our distress. Does anyone here come from a background of being involved in a religious organization?"

The room was still silent, but Jeremy raised his hand again and nodded his head.

"Many people believe that life is a gift from God," the chaplain explained. "And even though we will experience many hardships life can still be worth living. For centuries, many people have believed in a spiritual realm where a supreme being dwells, and we can talk to this God in prayer, asking for assistance."

Just then, Dale, a tall, thin, bearded, middle-aged man, abruptly stood up, and quickly exited the room. The group could hear him burst out in raucous laughter as he practically ran down the hallway. The remainder of the group squirmed in their seats.

"Alright, not everyone finds the idea of a god helpful; however, if we could set aside our doubts momentarily, perhaps the concept of faith in a higher power would be more agreeable than not," the chaplain said.

Just then, Betsy, a sarcastic brunette with hair sticking out in all directions, interjected: "But religion, especially, Christianity, has been so co-opted by the corrupt politicians that it's not worth pursuing anymore. At least, not for me. I don't want to be seen as associated with them so I keep my distance." She abruptly sneezed three times and got up to search for a box of Kleenex out at the nurses' station a few steps down the hall.

The chaplain waited a moment for Betsy to return and answered: "Yes, religion is sometimes misused and abused. Using religion with false motives such as for selfish, political gain is blasphemy. But God won't let them get away with anything. We have to answer to the higher power for all we think and do, answer to a God who sees all things and never sleeps. We are all accountable to this higher power."

Being mildly curious about the discussion the beautiful young woman suddenly stepped inside the room and hobbled over on her crutches to an empty chair and sat down.

"Welcome," the chaplain said.

A young man with boyish, wide eyes spoke up next: "I've done so many horrible things it's hard for me to imagine any kind of forgiveness coming from this God."

The chaplain had a ready response: "No matter how sinful we have been, God's grace is greater. God's mercy is very deep and wide. If we turn to God and say, 'I am sorry' or 'I repent,' we always get another chance at life."

The thick tension that had filled the room suddenly evaporated. Everyone began to breathe more abundantly and freely. Some patients sat up straighter in their chairs. But the beautiful young woman looked unconvinced and remained slouched over.

"Nope. Don't buy it," she mumbled softly, her head down, then she began rocking back and forth ever so gently.

Everyone turned and looked straight at her. One patient got up and walked over and patted the beautiful young woman on her shoulder. The beautiful young woman started weeping. No one had ever cared about her before, in a real way. She had only been used, mostly, for monetary gain. Now in this hospital, she felt for the first time the love of God. It was almost too much for her to bear and she felt incredibly embarrassed. She got up and left for her hospital room. Later, she put in a request for a private session with the chaplain.

Irene, a petite, freckled-faced, sandy-blond, twenty-something woman with rectangular black eye glasses, had been sitting quietly, just observing the group without saying a word. Her poker face had not registered any emotion. But deep inside, her thoughts and feelings were struggling to get out. Irene had been diagnosed with paranoid schizophrenia (not a split personality, but psychotic), and additionally diagnosed as a 2e person. As a 2e person, she was exceptionally bright, near genius, but also displayed a learning or intellectual disability near retardation in one or more areas. She excelled in complex problem solving and in writing creatively; but reading comprehension for such things as her school work was a big challenge which also fit in with being 2e. Irene could do well focusing on just one particular topic which captured her interest; but could not comprehend general areas of thought. Her inattention in social group gatherings, educational, and church activities were mistaken for laziness or indolence. However, she was incapable of paying attention due to her cognitive deficit. People judged her and ostracized her out of ignorance and prejudice.

Terri, another one in the session, was an exquisitely sensitive young woman. Her sense of smell, hearing, and touch were magnified. As a result, ordinary sights and sounds overwhelmed her. For example, she could not tolerate bright sunlight or loud lawn grooming machines outdoors. A lot of her free time was used in listening to beautiful, melodious music with earphones with her laptop or from her iPhone. This gave her some peace.

In an attempt to include everyone in the discussion the chaplain turned to Terri and invited her to express her ideas on the subject of faith.

"Hello, there, Terri. Do you have any thoughts about spirituality?"

Terri stirred uncomfortably in her chair and crossed one chubby leg over the other and then did the reverse. Her brow wrinkled and she frowned. Suddenly, her left hand went to her chest as a sharp pain radiated near her heart. She leaned slightly forward then slowly straightened. The discomfort left as quickly as it had arrived. Terri clasped both hands on her lap and after a moment her lips slightly moved, but no sound came out. She gently shook her head from side to side. Terri had been ignored for so many long years that she found it difficult to believe her ideas mattered at all. Why would anyone want to listen to her? It wasn't worth the effort.

The chaplain waited for about thirty seconds and then assumed that an answer would not be forthcoming, so she turned again to the whole group and asked another set of questions.

"So, everyone: how do we find friends? Where can we go to find friends?"

People had ideas such as the library or a chess club, a book group, gym, or a cooking class. The chaplain added that often we may find things in common with others in organizations such as a church or synagogue. Often, a religious organization will sponsor events that we can attend free of charge.

Next, the chaplain asked: "What gives us hope? What images come to mind? When do we feel the most zest for life? What motivates us and gives us the most energy? What are the reasons we want to live and what do we think our purpose is for living?"

Marvin, a heavyset, and quiet man in his early sixties, stirred in his seat, then tentatively raised his hand.

"Yes, Marvin, what would you like to say?" the chaplain asked.

I used to live for food, for eating. I'd wake up in the morning knowing donuts were waiting for me in the kitchen. I loved to eat them with my freshly-made coffee."

He stopped talking and his face blushed in embarrassment.

The chaplain, again, waited for more, but Marvin remained silent.

"Yes, food can be a prime motivation for living," the chaplain explained. "Without food, our bodies would die. Nothing wrong with craving food. It's just not good to be so obsessed with eating that other things become unimportant. Has anyone ever had a job they loved or some work that inspired them? How can we become inspired?"

No one in the circle responded, so the chaplain continued.

Perhaps a friend or mentor can inspire us. Has anyone ever had a teacher when growing up who seemed kind and special? Has there been a man or woman who took a special interest in you? Or have you felt ignored? Maybe you did not feel noticed growing up."

Again, silence. People seemed tired, so the chaplain decided to end the session for the day. All filed out of the room but one small, mouse-like woman who lingered and approached the chaplain. As she spoke in a whispering, soft voice the chaplain had to lean forward to hear her.

"The only time my mother spoke to me growing up was when she was angry about something. All my siblings bullied me. My father was largely absent because he had to work at several jobs to pay the bills. When one of my grandmothers babysat us, she beat me. The first time I ever felt love was in a church Sunday School class when I was about five years old. My friend invited me to come to the church with her. The teacher there said that God loves us and would take care of us like a shepherd would search until he found his lost sheep. So, this is all I have. I try to remember that God loves me like the shepherd."

She started weeping.

The chaplain, deeply touched, started to respond, but the small woman scurried out the door and down the hall sobbing.

3

Knitting With Barbed Wire

A NONDENOMINATIONAL RELIGIOUS ORGANIZATION invited guest speakers to preach once a month on Sunday mornings. They usually invited males but decided to experiment with a female speaker to see how it goes. They heard about the chaplain sister, her educational background in the philosophy of religion, and her successful work with the mentally ill in a near-by hospital. They sent her an invitation which she promptly accepted. The invitation specified that her sermon was to touch upon controversial theological controversies that plague churches (both ancient and modern-day) and social justice issues that tie into that. The chaplain sister thought this sounded rather broad and complicated so she responded that she would do what she could given the challenge of cohesion.

On the specified morning, a warm, bright, sunny day, the chaplain sister walked out to the center of a stage and took her place behind a medium-height oak wood podium. Her hair was tied back so not to interfere with her reading of notes. Looking out into the audience she saw people of all ages and of various dress, some casual, others more formal. She took a sip of water from the glass provided on a nearby table and cleared her throat. *This won't be easy*, she thought, *I'll do my best.*

She began.

Knitting with Barbed Wire

As noted in your bulletin my talk is titled: *Knitting With Barbed Wire*. Knitting with barbed wire is imagery to stimulate thought for a myriad of benevolent activities which at first appear beautiful and helpful, but in reality are an ugly exclusion and ostracization for those who are different—different in economic status, race, abilities, or expression, and who are clearly not welcome. The metallic, rusty, and sharp barbed wire emotionally, socially, and physically bars those deemed unwanted and any attempt by the excluded to rush through the wire results in severe cuts, deep injuries, and sometimes, death. Even in the church we can find barbed wire. Those who have lived a life of privilege and who are so self-absorbed in their personal pursuits that they exclude others—these people have created barriers. People from the other side of the tracks are foreign to the privileged and so often are ignored. Much gossip in the knitting circles reflect a callous-hearted disregard for those who suffer from poverty. "Why, they should be just thankful for what they've got!"

Barbed wire is all around, more so in some places than in others. It can put up barriers to keep the rich distant from the poor. It can deny others their basic human rights. What is the role and responsibility of religious communities in securing these basic rights? How do they fall short in today's world? The values of those who exclude others should be exposed for what they are. By reflecting upon Christ's teaching, we find means to achieving social equity in the hope of breaking down walls, removing barriers—the dismantling of barbed wire.

I will now mention a short excerpt about a man's life who truly knew suffering in this world. Sometimes it appears that barbed wire exists in the church separating the mentally ill from the rest of the people.

He stood alone in a room crowded with people. No one would approach him to converse. He wouldn't or couldn't move. He just stared straight ahead, motionless. Several times during his adult life he had be hospitalized for depression, but to no avail. With shock treatments, anti-depressant medications, and talk therapy, he still couldn't shake off the deep despair. Now elderly, he stood during fellowship time after worship in the atrium; but no one would chat with him. His loving wife went to get him a cup of coffee and I decided to approach him. I tried to strike up a conversation, but he only softly uttered one or two words. His depression seemed unsurmountable. His isolation unbearable. He was truly alone. Even though in the room there were about a hundred church members surrounding him, he could not mix. But it wasn't his own fault. He was spent. His efforts seemed futile to him now. He had tried so much for so long and had done so many things over the years to try to get well. Now, he just stood still.

Not long afterwards, the COVID 19 pandemic hit and took this man away. For all that knew him we hoped that this man in his suffering had found some relief. He was now in God's hands. Surely, he now had joy. This was our greatest hope for him. Joy, at last.

Somehow, the barbed wire separated this man from those around him who appeared to lead normal, happy lives. His distance from them was apparent and obvious. Why could they function socially, and he could not? His faith was strong and he loved Jesus. However, ever since the mental illness struck, people started to distance themselves from him.

How this is the case for all those with a mental illness! Once branded with a diagnosis, life is never the same. Sure, exceptions exist: that woman who offers transportation or mornings with coffee, donuts, and conversation. These types of friends are rare. The usual fare is the superficial smile and greeting on a Sunday morning that does not go any further. Why? People are afraid. Afraid that the mental illness could be contagious or that the mentally ill person will act out and do something inappropriate that would embarrass them. A few will take measures to self-educate themselves on the diagnosis, but most people are content with their ignorance and their own pre-existent circle of friends; they see no need to expand.

As another example of social exclusion, I will now tell you a short story about a non-white woman who experienced the barbed wire.

There was a Hispanic woman who shopped in a neighborhood grocery store. In the entrance of the store posters and flyers lined the wall. The woman noticed a flyer marketing a knitting group that gathered nearby every Saturday morning. The flyer said all are welcome to join the group. The woman wrote down the address and noted it was not in an area which was familiar to her. She decided to attend anyway that weekend to try it out.

As the woman drove her beige Kia up to the house she felt butterflies in her stomach. Having been brought up in a working-class family she saw that the knitting group met in a rather fancy, expensive house in an upscale neighborhood. But she decided to give it a try. Afterall, the flyer advertised that *All are Welcome!!* She parked her car and went up the winding sidewalk to ring the doorbell at the front entrance of the house. Soon a tall, stately, but frowning, older female with gray hair perfectly coiffed, opened the door and invited her inside. The Hispanic woman was ushered into a living room full of females of all age groups who were engaged in lively conversation as they worked on various knitting projects using colorful varieties of yarn. As she sat down on the only available chair, all eyes turned to her and the chattering abruptly halted. The woman, feeling slightly embarrassed, said softly, *Hello.*

Dead silence.

The group returned to their former position and resumed their knitting, chattering amongst one another.

The hostess invited the Hispanic woman to help herself to refreshments spread out on the dining room table nearby. As the woman approached the rectangular, wooden table covered with a white lace cloth, she saw a large pitcher of orange juice surrounded by tall stemmed Waterford handcrafted crystal goblets. The hostess poured the juice into a goblet and handed it to the woman. Cheese and crackers on a serving tray looked appetizing, so the Hispanic woman placed several pieces of food on a small black and white fez canapés plate and carried it along with her goblet back to her seat in the living room. She set the items on a high-gloss, white, STRAZ end table at the side of her chair. For the next few minutes, the woman munched on her snacks and, alternately, knitted a blue winter scarf she planned to donate to the Goodwill Store. Conversation buzzed all around her as needles clicked. At one point the hostess spoke, glancing up from her hands.

"You know, I've been thinking: I don't believe that disabled babies when born should be allowed to continue to live since they won't be able to support themselves financially when they grow up. They are just a burden on society! Useless eaters. Taking up valuable resources!"

The Hispanic woman knitting the scarf for Goodwill stopped, her mouth falling open. Frozen and staring in disbelief, she was shocked, speechless, and felt a growing, visceral fear. Images of her cousin, Anita, who had Down syndrome, flooded her mind and she suddenly felt compelled to say something in Anita's defense. Beginning softly, her voice quivered, then became strong and steady.

I want to say something to you! My dear, sweet cousin, who was born handicapped, now is living a purposeful and meaningful life, even with Down syndrome. She takes the bus on her own to her part time job at the lawn and garden store. Granted, she cannot afford to pay for all of her living expenses, but she is very human in every way, has friends, and loved ones. She loves and is loved—isn't that what life is all about? I disagree that they should be exterminated at birth. Just think of how you, yourselves, would want to be treated if you were in a car accident as a young adult or later on, and you lost a limb or suffered crippling aftereffects, even brain damage! Would you want people to think that you, yourselves, were then useless and needed to be exterminated? And, how about when you reach the senior years? Some of you are already there! Maybe you will need a wheelchair or will become bedridden. Many of us will need a home health aide. How would you feel if someone tried to exterminate you if you could no long function at full capacity—could no longer be employed or had severe limitations?

Suddenly, the room erupted with loud, angry outbursts, verbally assaulting the Hispanic woman in vicious tones.

"Where did you get your education, dear?"

"What field is your degree in?"

"Where do you get your information?"

Then the group bent forward to murmur amongst themselves, near to each other's faces. Occasionally, an audible word leaked out that the Hispanic woman could hear.

"*Ignorant.*"

"*Trash.*"

"*Uneducated!*"

The Hispanic woman caught her breath and quickly regained her composure. Unabated, she continued to address the group:

Yes, I'm from a lower-class family. I'm from the other side of the tracks—and a different culture. My parents were migrant farm workers and I'm not ashamed! They toiled in the hot sun like slaves, barely paid a day's wage, in deplorable conditions to provide your salads and fruit cocktail. They were abused, sometimes beaten, and often starving—nearly to death. But they were smart! They knew how to survive. They brought up their kids the right way, teaching self-discipline and good morals. They taught me to fear and revere God! I may not have made it to college, but I've studied on my own in libraries and have done research on-line—

A couple of women interjected.

"Oh, what do you know?!"

"Who brought you here, anyway?"

This last interruption and insult showed the woman that she was not going to get anywhere with this group. Even though the poster at the grocery store had declared that all are welcome in the knitting group, this was clearly not the case. The woman quickly gathered her things. All heads turned in her direction. Needles and yarn fell into laps as hands were stilled. The woman made her way to the door, without turning to say good-bye. This was not a friendly place. She felt terrified because there was such a chill in the air. As she got into her car a thunderstorm erupted in the morning sky and lightning flashed across the horizon. She drove herself home through a sudden downpour, a torrent of rain. Once in her apartment, she fell to her knees and pleaded with God to protect her. Never, had she experienced a colder, more callus group of strangers.

The chaplain paused a moment in her speech to allow the depth of the tragic story to sink in. After a few brief seconds, she continued.

We put up all kinds of barriers to keep out those who are disabled, or of a different culture or race, or who are self-educated. Some of us seem so narrow-minded in our outlook it's like we have blinders on. But God doesn't see people the same way we do. God looks at the heart. That overweight, poorly dressed, Black woman in the grocery store parking lot? Wasn't she the one who quickly dropped all her bags and immediately ran over to aid the elderly white man who slipped on the ice and broke a leg? Wasn't it she who, immediately, without hesitation, phoned the first responders asking them to help him? Isn't it those on the margins who surprise us with their compassion for others and heroic efforts? Those who've been excluded, either because of race, culture, or different-abilities—aren't they the ones who show us what it means to love?

I once had a college roommate who shared part of her life story with me. People may come from a background full of suffering. One cold winter night as we sat wrapped in our quilts while drinking tea during a bedtime chat, she told me the following:

I can't remember my mother ever hugging me. I do remember when I was a small child that my mother had metal cages on a table, all in a row, containing small, gray mice downstairs in the basement. Every day, following instructions from her college psychology professor, she conducted experiments according to Pavlov's conditioning theory of behaviorism. My mother became a follower of the behaviorist philosophy, i.e., the bait, reflex, reward, and bell theory. With such a materialist view that also applied to my own, human upbringing, I failed to encounter teachings on the value of introspection and contemplations of love and virtue, or other such traits for character formation, more of a depth psychology. If I did well in school my mother rewarded me by letting me bake a cake. If I did poorly, she wouldn't talk to me for a number of days as punishment or did so even less than usual. My mother rarely spoke. I never knew what was going on inside her head. The rest of my family was hyper-active who stormed about me, often knocking me down when I got in the way, if not physically, then verbally. I was physically and emotionally mistreated. When I was old enough this led me to find shelter in libraries, the corners in them where a solitary desk with chair allowed me to be quietly seated away from the crowds. I needed a quiet time and a space where I could gather my thoughts. This led to writing. As a teenager, I wrote lyrics to songs and music, teaching myself how to play the wooden recorder and guitar. But when I was away from home for a while, my dad sold my guitar without my knowledge. This was devastating. I decided to major in clinical psychology now in college in order to help others.

The roommate continued. If anything good can be said about hardship, one is this: It teaches us to go down from the surface to look deeper for meaning in life, it directs us away from the maddening crowd. However, my parents did do something great. Once in a while they brought my siblings and I to church; so that was an incredibly good thing. I remember how beautiful the church building was, the sunshine streaming through the stain glass windows, the hymns-singing. In Sunday school we got treats of cookies and Kool-aide, how I enjoyed that. Good memories. Then, back home after worship, it was the same type of trials again. But the experience of a religious community gave me some strength and direction. The effects from the experience of being in a church worshipping God was something that never left me and I continued to carry with me my entire adult life. I think though, that, unfortunately, if a child is not brought up in a religious community this can be detrimental for their entire lifespan.

The chaplain, reaching the end of that story, continued.

Now on a different matter. Even though there are certainly a lot of power games in the church, especially between men and women, sometimes, a woman can find assistance in her research from male scholars. I have encountered a great deal of theological pluralism in my Protestant church which I disagree with and I see it as a huge problem This is not new but has existed for over a millennium world-wide. Phil Cary, Emeritus Prof of Philosophy, Eastern University; Editor, Pro Ecclesia: A Journal of Catholic and

Evangelical Theology, is one male who is helpful. On the subject of pluralism, he states the following:

Pluralism is one of the most common ways for institutions and churches to go post-Christian these days. It's one thing to recognize the reality of different religions and respect people who are unlike you. It's another thing altogether to talk as if every religion is equally true. To take that second track is to abandon Christian faith, which has a very specific message to give to the world, centered on the uniqueness of Jesus Christ.

The irony is that to give up on the uniqueness of your own religion is reduce the diversity in the world. Pluralism does not in fact honor difference but makes everybody look the same (they're all equally true, etc.). No real religion believes that. So pluralism turns out to be a way of denying that different religions are unique and different. It is really a form of modern Western intellectual imperialism.[1]

For there is one God and one mediator between God and men, the man Christ Jesus, who gave himself as a ransom for all men. (1 Timothy 2:5–6a NIV)

Most of the people who advocate for pluralism have no inkling of what the other world religions are comprised of. They have not studied them and are blissfully ignorant. For example, Buddhism is an atheist religion. And Hinduism is not monotheistic, they believe in many gods, including divine animals. Islam sees the person of Jesus Christ as something other than God's son who is the Messiah. Jesus cannot be both the Messiah (Christianity) and not the Messiah (Islam) at the same time. And as far as the atheist religions: I want to ask people: how can a religion that does not believe there is a God (Buddhism) be equal to a monotheistic religion like Christianity that believes in a God? And how can these two theologies as a theoretical reality co-exist at the same time? It's impossible! Either there is a God or not; you can't have it both ways simultaneously. And with Hinduism, how can it be true that there be many gods when Christianity says there is only one monotheistic God? One or the other religion is true: these two religions cannot exist simultaneously. You can only accept one or the

---

1. Phil Cary, email to author, 3/14/2023.

other, not both at the same time. The trouble is compounded, then, with the more diverse religions you add on. The lack of conscience by denying intellectual integrity is profound in pluralism. People who call themselves Christian deny the centrality and uniqueness of Christ all the time without feeling any guilt. There is no sense of *intellectual* right and wrong; no rational integrity. But these very same people, the pluralists, often, very lovingly, and with great determination, uphold justice issues and show the compassion of Christ. This is a conundrum. For example, there may be a pluralist who takes in a homeless woman into her home, offering shelter, when the Christian man (or who claims to be Christian) turns his back on all the unsheltered.

I need to point out that the Interfaith movement, based on relativism and pluralism, is complacent. It is accepting the insanity, the irrationality, of pluralism as though everything is just fine, so let's set up the soup kitchen for the poor together while ignoring the seriousness of the theological contradictions. Soup kitchens are good and necessary and joint efforts are, indeed, needed; however, we can't just relax and say all is fine theologically. Eternal lives are at stake; there's an urgency here. Except for Universalism, where some believe that all souls will eventually end up in God's kingdom—eternity, taught biblically, will either be in a divine heaven or one is lost in the realm of unsaved souls. Education on the issues is essential and dialogue should delve into theological differences to understand matters rationally. Basing our lives on false premises is the path to destruction both while alive on earth and in the afterlife.

Then Jesus came to them and said, "All authority in heaven and on earth has been given to me." (Matt 28:18 NIV)

You shall have no other gods before me. (Exodus 20:3 NIV)

The previous Bible verses clearly state that all authority has been given to Christ. You either believe that, or you don't. You can't have it both ways. Buddha is not the authority, or the main figures in the other world religions. This is either true or false and the side you take will fundamentally determine your mental health. Why do I say this? The reasons are as follows.

I want to refer you to Chapter Four of *Reflections on the Meaning of Mental Integrity: Recovery from Serious Mental Illness*, titled: *Mental Illness in World Cultures*.[2] You see, mental illness is world-wide and exists in any culture, place, or time. This cannot be denied. It is everywhere. So, what causes mental illness? And is there a universal cure? Since there are many kinds of mental illness, I do not want to cause confusion, but will focus now on one primary problem, the *psychosis*.

During a psychosis an individual may experience what science calls, hallucinations, the hearing of voices or thoughts that intrude in the mind. There can be other forms of hallucinations as well. Most likely, it is an evil torment and causes distress; though there are also experiences of comfort at times with some people. Whether the voices are directly within the head or in the outside environment surrounding the person, the effect is similar. Modern Western society has purported the importance of neuroleptic medications in the era of the broken brain. This has been helpful, though incomplete. I propose that the broken brain is part of the equation in a holistic view in treating the psychosis but not the entire story. See *Voices in the Rain: Meaning in Psychosis*[3] for how this issue is addressed in full.

Where does Jesus, the Christ, fit in? Christ, as ultimate authority, has the spiritual power with which to defeat all evil forces. My Roman Catholic friends are more familiar with this view. For centuries, the priest has played a dominant role in exorcisms to heal those afflicted with evil spirits or devils and demons. There are nonfiction publications that chronical such episodes and stories. See Appendix D, "Resources on the Reality of Spiritual Conflict," in the book, *Reflections on the Meaning of Mental Integrity.*[4] We cannot deny that evil exists as we survey the everyday world around us. Demonic forces impose all kinds of difficulties whether it be in social situations or in a broader ideological sense. Or closer to home, just reflect on the casual, daily encounter with our own

---

2. Murphy, *Reflections Mental Integrity*, 42–59.
3. Murphy, *Voices in the Rain*.
4. Murphy, *Reflections Mental Integrity*, 88–89.

small voices we combat within our consciousness. *No, I'd better not do that. Yes, this is a good decision, not the other.* Sometimes, there is a foreign, strange thought—where did it come from? Consciousness is a mixture of random, complex ideas and impulses. It would be beneficial to have the spiritual force of the Almighty on our side to do battle against the malevolent and negative.

This is why daily, morning prayer is so very important. First, I start my day with scripture reading, specifically, the Bible. I read parts of both the New Testament and the Old. I start with the Gospel, Jesus's words. I go on to the Epistles, and end with the Psalms and prophets' admonitions and comforts. Without this beginning to my day, I'd be lost. People who have experienced life-long psychosis particularly need this strong religious stance. Christ is the defender, so praying the Lord's Prayer along with other supplications in the morning is very helpful.

One of the reasons I deeply care about this theological issue of pluralism is because good mental health requires thinking in logical ways and logic, when properly understood, incorporates truth. I maintain that truth in theological belief is essential for good mental health. The more irrational a person's thought patterns become the more mentally ill and delusional. To be irrational in the extreme is complete insanity. Churches need pastors who will stand up for truth and the biblical way of understanding the world. A biblical worldview is also essential to successfully navigate the outer world. Though there will always be substantial barriers and challenges to overcome, a rational human being is better off than the irrational one. People who have mental health issues especially need a pastor who is logical and who has the integrity to preach the truth. When we hear the truth through a logical pastor's sermon, this greatly influences our mental well-being. Inversely, hearing chaotic narrative or speech of irrationality is detrimental for our mental health. What we hear or listen to, matters, and has further implications and consequences for our lives.

The chaplain continued.

And while I'm at it, here is another controversial issue rampant in the church: the LGBTQ question. First off, I want to make it perfectly clear that I strongly believe that all people of any identity choice should be welcomed into the Christian church. I believe in full social inclusion of all people, as *all* are loved by God and we need to love one another regardless of our differences. However, it is my opinion that LGBTQ lifestyles and identities may, in some cases, lead to mental illness as well as religious idolatry. People may obsess with the issue, making it the main focus of their life, instead of placing God first. I also believe that marriage is only between one biological male and one biological female; this is how we were physically created and is also biblically sanctioned. The Bible is clear: (Rom 1:24–27 ESV). When same-sex partners engage in sexual acts this can cause devastating injuries (both physical and emotional) that can last a lifetime. It is evident that only a man and a woman were made to be together, not the other way around.

There are some secular and religious organizations that may try to impose a censorship of these stated views. In some parts of the country and world there may not be freedom of speech, including in some religious organizations. Any organization in the US, whether of the Left or Right, which imposes restriction of expression for opinions on these issues is fascist and dictatorial.

Continuing on, now, what about the question of tradition and dogma?

When people criticize the idea of religious tradition or criticize the practice of following religious tradition, they are, at the same time, just putting another type of tradition in its place be it atheistic or agnostic, so everyone is basically following some kind of tradition but they just won't admit it. No one was raised in a vacuum, empty nothingness. We all are influenced by our social environment. The psychological literature clearly describes how things are not what they seem. We hope to be independent thinkers; however, influences abound which we cannot escape. We are all products of the great influencers around us, be it atheist or religious. True, at times, we make choices. This is why God clearly says that we will be judged for the good or evil we do. And the freedom we experience will allow a voluntary, loving response to the Creator of the world—which is our purpose in life. And when people say dogma is horrible, they are really just soaked in their own dogmatic believes anyway. We all have our own dogmas and are living out one kind of dogma whether of scientific/materialistic, or theological, or political/ideological.

Dogma and tradition can be used interchangeably. The worldviews we hold, the beliefs we adhere to, this is our own dogma or choice in what kind of thought tradition we accept. Tradition and dogma are concepts that extend far beyond theology; they just are words to describe our own personal choices in lifestyles and values which, by the way, did not pop up out of nothingness, but, instead, are partly derived from many influential sources experienced within our personal and social histories.

Concerning the topic of tradition, Phil Cary states: *Everybody lives, acts, thinks and feels within some tradition or other—and in the modern world, it's often many traditions, like scientists who go to church. Each of the sciences has its own tradition, as do the churches. The traditions can be rational, self-critical, and learn new things, as well as be faithful to old, well-established truth. And they can also be subject to conflict and revision.*[5]

Going on to another matter, many church pastors and members ask about a puzzling biblical event: Why was Jesus Christ baptized? People try to discredit Christ because he was baptized, but Phil Cary teaches that:

Jesus was certainly human but he was not sinful. This is precisely why John the Baptist hesitated to baptize him. "I need to be baptized by you," he said, " and you come to me?" (Matt 3:14 ESV). Far from being a sinner, he is, John says, the one who takes away the sins of the world (John 1:29 ESV). So Jesus has to persuade him to go ahead and baptize him. In the Gospels Jesus doesn't say exactly why he wants John to do this, but I think we can see what's up. The meaning of baptism is a kind of re-inauguration. When we get baptized today, we are born again. Earlier, when John was baptizing at the Jordan, it was a kind of re-inauguration of Israel's identity, retracing their entry into the Promised Land as they crossed Jordan River. John

---

5. Phil Cary, email to author, 3/14/2023.

wants to renew Israel, and in Christ all things have become new, and Jesus is in fact leading the way into the ultimate Promised Land. For us sinners, that requires repentance. For him, it required the humility of taking on flesh so that he may die for us. But the Father testifies from heaven that he is well-pleased with this incarnate Son of his. (John 1:29–34 ESV)[6]

*

So, there are many religious questions and issues encountered on a person's spiritual journey, both for those with relatively good health and also those with mental afflictions; and we need to be educated on all sides of the issues to help us sort out our own beliefs.

In my final words I will share a lament. It appears that some individuals who are dependent on others in their religious community in many cases have to sacrifice their own personal intellectual and spiritual freedoms in order to be considered socially included and, tragically, in order to be able to access vital material or financial resources necessary for survival. Unfortunately, forceful coercion and bullying in religious communities is not unheard of. As such, there is spiritual exile of individuals in a land of plenty. I maintain, however, that as stated in the United Nations's Universal Declaration of Human Rights that there should be:

> Freedom of thought and religion. Everyone has the right to freedom of thought, conscience, and religion; this right includes freedom to change his religion or belief, and freedom, either alone or in community with others and in public or private, to manifest his religion or belief in teaching, practice, worship, and observance.
>
> Freedom of opinion and expression. Everyone has the right to freedom of opinion and expression; this right includes freedom to hold opinions without interference and to seek, receive, and impart information and ideas through any media and regardless of frontiers.

---

6. Phil Cary, email to author, 3/14/2023.

Right to assemble. Everyone has the right to freedom of peaceful assembly and association. No one may be compelled to belong to an association.[7]

The chaplain stopped and took a good look at the audience, scanning the whole room. It was silent. She gathered her papers in one hand and spoke clearly:

Thank you for listening.

She walked off the stage.

---

7. Universal Declaration of Human Rights, *30 Basic Human Rights List*, 5.

4

No Place to Call Home

AS THE CHAPLAIN CONTINUED her work on the psych wards, she learned that some patients give up living in their apartments because it is not really a home. They feel so isolated and it is too much to bear. They'd rather be out on the streets with their friends, their buddies. But that gets them, eventually, into trouble again. It's a revolving door. The government policies punish those who are trying to make it out of poverty; there are no incentives. The homeless and disabled usually are not allowed companions who can live with them, friends to talk to, and eat meals with. The nights get very long. Individuals rarely enjoy staying in a single apartment unit by themselves because the apartment feels like a prison cell.

There is not enough affordable housing. There are many construction sites erecting luxury condos and other high-end buildings for those who have a lot of money. The government's housing voucher system in this area has over 10,000 people on their waiting list to get assistance (2024). That list is now closed for several years in order to whittle it down. The housing assistance is currently helping hundreds, so that is good. Even though homeless shelters are not ideal for every type of person, they do great work, and continuous funding for more of these types of emergency services are needed.

How do people become homeless? One example is the hard-working mother of four, who worked thirty years in a factory job only to become disabled and in need of surgery. Then there is the couple who had an emergency medical problem that took all their savings. There is the parents of a disabled child who had special needs and time requirements. Illness, late rent, evictions. Some had predatory neighbors who threatened their lives so they had to escape in the dark of night. Some people couldn't shake alcohol abuse and the drinking patterns learned during youthful days. Some people were born into poverty, never had enough to eat, and could not concentrate in school so then flunked out, only to be denied employment or who did find a job but was not provided a living wage.

Some churches have made great strides in helping the poor and those who are oppressed. They are fulfilling Christ's mandate expressed in scripture (Matthew 25:34–40 NIV). *"Then the King will say to those on his right, 'Come, you who are blessed by my Father; take your inheritance, the kingdom prepared for you since the creation of the world. For I was hungry and you gave me something to eat, I was thirsty and you gave me something to drink, I was a stranger and you invited me in I needed clothes and you clothed me, I was sick and you looked after me, I was in prison and you came to visit me.'*

"Then the righteous will answer him, 'Lord, when did we see you hungry and feed you, or thirsty and give you something to drink? When did we see you a stranger and invite you in, or needing clothes and clothe you? When did we see you sick or in prison and go to visit you?'

"The King will reply, 'Truly I tell you, whatever you did for one of the least of these brothers and sisters of mine, you did for me.'"

And the congregants in worship services hear:

Suppose a brother or a sister is without clothes and daily food. If one of you says to them, "Go in peace; keep warm and well fed," but does nothing about their physical needs, what good is it? In the same way, faith by itself, if it is not accompanied by action, is dead. (James 2:15–17 NIV)

Sometimes, being unsheltered may feel that knitting with barbed wire refers to using whatever resources are available to create an item. If a person is stuck in poverty, soft, pretty yarn is unavailable. Instead, we use whatever strands of wire we find, pieces from the homeless encampment fencing. Wires entangled, stabbing, and cold, prohibiting advancement into the city to find warm, hospitable shelter.

As the chaplain reflected on all these points she thought to herself that most of the Christians she personally knew were compassionate human beings who made a big difference in other's lives. They really care about others who need assistance and are God's instruments on earth. The chaplain thought that just saving money for yourself will not make you successful. No amount of money can give you good, loving relationships of depth or, what is supremely important, how to know and love God. So, Western culture has it all backwards. It is built on capitalism, dog eat dog, competition, and profit. No wonder the violence, political corruption, and moral decay. People are seeking happiness in material goods, food, sex, power, and control. The church exists in contrast to this sick society. The church gives people a nonmaterial reason to live. The church teaches Christian principles and provides direction so people won't flounder, or go off in wild, self-centered directions. The church, which is accountable to God, is Christ's light in a dark, brutal world.

The chaplain spent some time praying and asking God for answers. She thought of a colleague of hers who had written a book on the homelessness problem, featuring one unsheltered man. This woman had spent years researching the causes and possible solutions. The shelters were a big help; but there are always homeless people still sleeping on the sidewalks downtown because the shelters were full or intolerable because of over-crowding, commotion, and mistreatment due to mental health or substance abuse issues. Those without shelter who are sleeping on the sidewalks downtown in all kinds of weather are also sometimes physically assaulted, being vulnerable to all kinds of abuse. But there are some people who do care and personally welcome a homeless person into their home and provide what the individual needs to survive. The church is responding to this great need and is God's hand at work in the world.

However, once a homeless or low-income person can find housing in their own apartment, what kind of living conditions are they subjected to? Sometimes, the neighbors in the building are bullies and these bullies inflict horrendous abuse. This mistreatment is especially prevalent against the disabled, mentally, and/or physically. There are next door neighbors who appear to lack a conscience with no sense of right or wrong. It seems they are obsessed with bullying, and make it their life goal to torture the disabled tenant next door, daily.

Ableism is discrimination and social prejudice against people with physical or mental disabilities. Ableism characterizes people as they are defined by their disabilities and it also classifies disabled people as people who are inferior to non-disabled people.[1]

There once was an autistic young man, rather meek and physically, very weak and extremely thin, bony, his hair always in disarray and his smudged eye glasses askew. He could be seen riding to his job on the city bus, his head buried into a thick paperback book. He kept to himself. Even at work, a local burger joint, he would periodically disappear into a darkened, back room to fix the sandwiches when a particular customer spooked him. All was taken in stride by his coworkers and they thanked him for making the sandwich as he re-entered the front room. They knew of his disability and extreme sensitivity.

So, this man lived in an apartment building which housed eleven other tenants. There was one tenant, a woman, who made it her life mission to torment the autistic man on a daily basis. Whenever he went down to the mailbox in the lower hallway, she would open her apartment door and yell obscenities at him and threaten him. She would on other occasions tear his name label off his mailbox when it is a federal crime to hamper with the mailboxes and he needed his name visible to receive his mail from the postal carrier. Other times, the woman would spit at his mailbox and still

---

1. Wikipedia, *Ableism*, para 1.

again, would spit on his apartment door. She also put saliva in his security peep hole or at times use a black ink marker. Blocking the visibility of this security hole was a violation of his rights because it was a dangerous neighborhood, a high crime area, and this visual aid was important for his safety.

Not only this, but the woman would also walk by his apartment door any time of the day or night, and swing a chain or other heavy object to bash against his door. One time, she pounded on his door with her fists as though to break it down. The autistic man never felt safe and was too disabled to inform the police. Even when this woman banged on the kitchen walls and tormented him by slamming her cupboards violently, there was nothing he could do. Once he did try to call the police, but they dismissed his complaints without an investigation telling him he couldn't prove the allegations. At times, when he tried to bathe and take showers, the woman next door would harass him by pounding on the bathroom walls. He never had any peace.

The next-door bully would gossip with the neighbors and he could hear her speaking lies about him in the hallway. Once he heard a small child screaming and yelling from her living room. He heard raucous laughter and violence of physical altercations, crashing of furniture with someone yelling, *No, no!*

The autistic man had been brought up in the Christian religion that taught him to love his enemies, so one day he put a grocery store gift card worth $25 at her door with a small box of chocolates. Still, to no avail, the abuse continued. The woman appeared to lack a conscience or any sense of civility. She appeared to have a demonic personality out to destroy others.

This is the type of thing disabled people have to put up with and their very lives are at risk. The autistic man also overheard the woman next door talking to a man in her apartment about *making a hit*, that she promised him cash if he'd do away with someone.

There was also a poverty-stricken woman who was disabled, both mentally and physically. Her biological family neglected her severely and the government disability benefits were not enough for her survival. She never had enough food. She made frequent trips to the crisis center's food bank. She also went to a foodbank in her neighborhood. The lab tests at her medical care appointments showed she suffered from malnutrition. Once a well-off church acquaintance visited her in her home to share coffee and conversation. The poor woman opened her kitchen cupboard to show one small can of tuna fish on the shelf in her otherwise bare cupboard. The poor woman laughed and said to the friend: "Isn't that hysterical?" The friend said nothing then, but soon after made sure the poor lady had all the food she needed.

Another church member soon started a food distribution program for the poor in the surrounding area. Showing the love of Christ, she is helping the hungry with a generous heart. Her program, with several dozen volunteers, feeds hundreds of families and individuals every month. The Spirit moves throughout the church.

5

Importance of God for Mental Health

THE CHAPLAIN SISTER WAS exhausted. Her first year of clinical work on the psychiatric units and speaking engagements took their toll. It was difficult and she felt drained. She decided to take some time off to do some research for a book project. Her supervisor, valuing the chaplain's contributions was agreeable, and allowed the chaplain six months leave. The chaplain wanted to search out answers to the following questions: What is the impact of long-term religious belief on a person's cognitive functioning? Also, on their emotions, and behaviors?

For part of her research the chaplain purchased an old-fashioned micro-tape recorder with tapes and set to work. She chose acquaintances and friends from her church, individuals who had exemplary character. Doing one-on-one interviews the chaplain set out to find answers to some questions related to faith. She also mailed out questionnaires, asking for replies. From the chaplain's point of view, they all seemed like rather healthy human subjects to examine. What were some of the factors related to their good mental health and strong character?

The chaplain found some pretty insightful responses and, in the text, left the participants as anonymous. The title of her work-in-progress was: *The Importance of God for Mental Health: A Preliminary Study*. These are the questions the chaplain asked:

1. Were you involved in a church or religious community at a young age? If so, what are your earliest recollections of the experience? How important was it to you as a youngster?
2. Was there an important person(s) in your life who helped you or guided you? Describe this person(s) and how they shaped your life.
3. What major events shaped your life or gave your life purpose? Are you satisfied with your life's trajectory?
4. How important has God and/or religion been in your lifetime (or at various stages of your life)?
5. What helps you get through difficult times? What do you rely on? Who or what do you turn to?

For the sake of contrast the chaplain also included analyses in her project the negative side, people who endured turmoil and strife in their up-bringing. Her work on the psych units showed examples of severe suffering as some families had parents who had problems and got divorced leading to difficulties with the children. One mother, for a period of approximately forty years, was in an adulterous relationship with a married man and neither of them tried to hide the fact from relatives or friends. Though the chaplain was not sure of a connection, this woman's family eventually experienced what appeared to be supernatural demonic activity and events within their home, terrifying the children. As such, there were parents who did not teach ethical ways or maintain moral discipline. They abused alcohol and some pornography. Few words of guidance were spoken to help children on their way and, instead, harsh language was screamed in emotional violence, even obscenities. There was not only psychological abuse but physical, also. Name-calling damaged the mental health of the siblings and no adult authority figure would intervene in defense of the child who was bullied. The bullying in some home environments was rampant, severe, and daily. Children did not know the love of God and it seemed that parents were to blame. But these same parents had experienced identical problems when they were growing up and were just continuing the unhealthy cycle. Some parents focused mainly on money and romance or sports and entertainment. Without good role models and examples to follow, the children drifted off into God-less relationships and occupations that caused not only harm to themselves, but to strangers. The children did not flourish, but floundered in adulthood. Many were suicidal.

The counterpoint would be strong, healthy individuals and families. Granted, no family is perfect; there are always some flaws. But the chaplain found that some people do have factors in common that facilitate healthy lifestyle choices along with the establishment of good marriages. The chaplain decided to quote the survey participants directly, to use their own words. The exceptions were editorial corrections done for the sake of clarity. For all stories that follow, the reader is to refer back to the questions as listed above.

MALE PHYSICIAN AND MEDICAL MISSIONARY

I was involved in a church as far back as I can remember because my Dad was a pastor, and we were at Sunday School and church [worship services] every Sunday. My earliest recollections were hearing Dad preach, sitting with Mom in the pew, and singing in the children's choir. It was very important because our lives revolved around church.

My parents were the most important people who guided me. My Dad was not only a good preacher, but he also lived out his faith. I had no doubts about the sincerity of his or my Mom's faith. He disciplined me when I needed it, but he also showed me what grace is. My mother did more of the day-to-day guidance, teaching, and discipline. Both Mom and Dad were regular in our prayers at meals and bedtime.

When I went off to a state university, I was surrounded by people and experiences that made me question my faith. I had to struggle with that, but by that struggle with God, and with myself—during a time when I had no meaning or purpose in my life—I discovered a deeply personal relationship with Jesus. And when I gave my heart and will over to him completely, I found the meaning and purpose that I was so desperately looking for—loving Christ and loving people.

God has been very important to me throughout the different stages of my life. As a child and adolescent, my parents taught and showed me what God was like, and gave me a model of living. God gave me these faith-filled parents. During my years of college struggle with faith, God taught me and loved me into faith by sending people my own age who had deep, personal faith in Christ. And in my adult life, God has led, guided, and strengthened me for his service.

God is my refuge and my strength in difficult times (and in easier times). I rely on him daily for his wisdom, guidance, peace, and hope—even when things don't look good. He is my shepherd, the lover of my soul. There is no one I would trust with my heart and soul more than Jesus.

FEMALE PHYSICIAN, MEDICAL MISSIONARY

My parents were faithful church-goers throughout my growing up years, often singing in the choir, and active in the church. I remember singing hymns by them and attending a lot of potlucks at church. I remember at age eight starting to repeat the lines of the pastor's prayers. I remember the prayers being long, and I said to myself that I needed to actually *pray them* to feel more connected to God. We also went to church camps at times. My parents didn't talk about faith at home and didn't often pray before meals, but church and community was important!

Our pastor during my 7th to 12th grade years was an important guide in my younger faith journey. He was young, energetic, and related to youth well, calling us to be *radically honest* with God. He even told me when I was about fourteen that I was going to be a medical missionary, much to my chagrin (I didn't have a good feeling about missionaries at the time, but I don't know why). He encouraged us and gave opportunities for service projects frequently. Also, a person in the church choir in 1979 encouraged me to go on a medical mission trip. I went to the Dominican Republic that summer and met my husband on the trip (married, six years later), and my eyes were opened to the needs of people internationally.

On my third try, I was accepted into the UI Med School and felt privileged to become a family physician. Friends along the way opened my eyes to the world of medical missions and offered a very meaningful purpose for my life. I am satisfied with the way God led me/us in life.

God became *real* to me when I was approximately eight years old and helped to shape my motivation for service and a meaningful career. During my husband's and my years of raising three children—first overseas and then in Kentucky—I was very active in faith communities but spent little time in personal growth with God. *Too busy!* But in the next phase of life, working in South Sudan and since being evacuated in 2016, and onward, I have grown in my faith and reliance on God (not self). My morning devotional time is richer and important to me, and I long to share God's love and grace with my family (and grandchildren) and others.

My faith in a loving, merciful God helps me through difficult times, as well as good Christian friends and family. I/We have been privileged to spend a lot of time with friends from around the world who pray for me/us and speak love and care into our lives. Fellowship with like-minded followers of Jesus help me to grow in my faith through the difficulties life brings.

ANONYMOUS FEMALE

Yes, I was involved in a church. I remember times there since I was five or six years old. It was very important to me. My grandma was very important to me. She was stern but always there, and made me feel safe. The church camp and my high school job were major events that shaped my life and gave my life purpose. I am very satisfied with my life. God has been important to me as a child, and as an adult. What helps me get through difficult times is my faith and belief that everything has a purpose and can lead to good.

ANONYMOUS FEMALE

I recall being involved in church when we moved to Bethesda, Maryland, and I was in the 5th grade. I had attended Sunday School in Evanston, Ill. very occasionally. I had a positive experience from 5th grade on, throughout High School. The youth pastor was active and innovative, and my various Sunday School teachers were conscientious and knowledgeable. VBS [Vacation Bible School] was good, and we older ones were encouraged to participate in meaningful ways i.e., helping with presenting messages and printing a daily newsletter. In High School, as classmates, we quickly bonded even more through weekly Youth Group activities i.e., studying scripture, having fun times i.e., ping pong, service projects, Christmas caroling, etc.

My parents were good, honest people who loved us. Several Sunday School teachers who were especially knowledgeable of scripture and encouraged scripture memory, and the youth pastor mentioned above, impacted my life as well. I remember a friend and I walked to school together, and we would talk about being missionaries together when we grew up. (5th-6th grade) Being the youth rep on a Pastor Nominating Committee gave me some spiritual insight.

Being the oldest of four children gave me a sense of responsibility early on, as did walking to the nearby grocery market for bread and milk when we lived in Illinois. There were some High School honors and I was elected HS Chaplain of our senior class of approximately 500. In High School I enjoyed going to the nearby Baptist church for Lenten services. The landmarks of going off to college, family tent camping trips in US, and one in Europe, college and graduate studies, marriage to the love of my life, the birthings and raising of five children were all major events. As parents, we took our family tent camping at many of the National Parks in the US. Joining Bible Study Fellowship after a neighbor persisted in inviting me prompted me to realize at an even deeper level what it meant for Jesus to be my Lord and Savior. I was busy and resistant at first, but the experience was life giving, and I eventually became the Substitute Teaching Leader. Husband Don going to heaven in 2020 was yet another life shaping event. Service has also been a continuous strand through the years. I never exactly put my *purpose* into words. *I looked to the Lord for my strength*, always felt loved, and sought to love and care for others, and do my best . . . living out the Golden Rule, and *To act justly, and to love mercy, and to walk humbly with your God* (Micah 6:8 NIV) is what I strive to do.

God has been of key importance to me from 5th grade to the present. The joy of the Lord is my strength and my song. Now that my husband is not walking beside me, though he is in my heart, I have become even more dependent on God's guidance and guarding. Morning devotions, spiritual readings, morning, and evening prayer structure my life. My time is my own—and I need to make wise choices.

ANONYMOUS MALE

I was not involved in a church as a youth. I always looked up to my Dad and my maternal grandfather. Both were well-liked. Neither offered a lot of advice, but I learned some things by watching. The major events that shaped my life were graduating from college, getting married, and having children. I am satisfied with my life's trajectory. Religion has not been at the forefront of my life, but has been reliably there. When I have difficult times, my faith is part of what helps me; and I find that people help me the most.

ANONYMOUS FEMALE

I remember going to church pot lucks when I was four or five. My parents attended church, but talked little about faith when home. I went without thinking about it. During confirmation, in Junior

High, the leader spoke about his faith, and I was surprised at his sharing, and his conviction. His deep faith was new to me.

I don't think I ever had a mentor. I looked up to my parents, and recognized qualities such as kindness, organization, cheerfulness, that they embodied and I have tried to emulate. But I know their faults too, rigid, self-important, that shaped me too; but I didn't want to be like that.

Some major events were a divorce, going to Haiti, having children, jobs I got (or didn't get). Purpose is an inner drive, believing that what is being done is worthwhile. That I love and am loved, and what I do will make life better. I try not to dwell on choices after they are made. My life's trajectory may have been altered if my choices had been different; but I am content with where I am.

God knows my religious uncertainties. I envy the person who feels that God is with them at every moment (to the point that their day is like a constant prayer), but I don't believe that I comprehend God that well. I do believe that there is a God and he is good and loving. I'm not sure I can separate how my belief has impacted my life choices. To get me through difficult times, I pray. I lean on friends. I remind myself that this is one period in a (hopefully) long life, and I will get past this.

FEMALE PHYSICIAN

I attended mass with my family for as long as I can remember. I also remember leaving the Catholic school after 6th grade which was a good decision for me. Both of my parents guided me in secular, as well as religious things. They showed me how we can appreciate God's love for us through enjoying nature and putting friends in our lives. Leaving the Catholic school, the Catholic church, and then finding a new church community that strives to be inclusive, encourages learning. A visit to the Philippines during high school impacted my professional life and gave me purpose in serving others. I am satisfied with my life's trajectory. God has been important at times, more important during other times. God, our Creator, has always been important but the man-made church or organized religion has sometimes impeded my relationship with God and with others. Prayers and friends help me get through difficult times.

ANONYMOUS FEMALE

When I was a child my family was faithful to the local Methodist church. Both parents taught Sunday School; we were always expected to go and it was a *way of life*. It was reassuring to have a strong faith and I have always been grateful to my parents for this early instruction.

The important persons who guided me were obviously my parents. They lived their faith and were honest, giving folks. They taught by example! I was the eldest of four girls born in four years so we needed lots of guidance and certainly received it along with high expectations for how we would live our lives. I admired both of my parents but, certainly, my Mother was a strong example for me. My parents were both educated as teachers, but I decided I wanted to be a nurse and they approved, so I proceeded with my education. I secured a BSN and then an MA in Nursing Administration. It has been very fulfilling for me because teaching, giving, helping others, and assisting with healing have been a strong purpose in my life. I was able to guide the department of nursing for fourteen years. It is something I can still do even in my *old age*, although not professionally because my health isn't the best. I always felt guided by my loving God for providing the pathway for me.

God has always been central to my life. I pray daily and depend on him. I suspect like many others I am more fervent in my prayers when I am hurting or afraid, lose someone important in my life or have special needs. I know he is always there and I am not hesitant to ask no matter what the circumstances. I've experienced many difficult times and struggled with major losses during my eighty-nine years on earth. I've relied on my loving God, my family, and dear friends. They always come through and I try to do the same for others. Sometimes I have to be quiet and listen and be aware of what and where my help might come. I've also learned to be patient with myself, whether in physical pain or emotional pain. It isn't easy nor am I good at it, but I keep trying! I know God hears my requests and I have faith things will work out for the best.

ANONYMOUS FEMALE

My grandfather was a Methodist minister, so I was baptized as an infant. However, my earliest memory of church was after World War II, when my father returned from Japan. We moved from Huston, to Denton, to be near my aging paternal grandparents. I was taken to Sunday School and I saved every Sunday School paper I was given, binding them into a book. I didn't want to miss a single Sunday because I would miss getting a Sunday School paper. This was in third grade.

My maternal grandmother who I called *Ga-ga*, was a Southern lady originally from North Carolina. Although she was an invalid when I knew her, she impressed upon me behavior: *Ladies don't smoke!* She also quoted favorite Bible verses and explained them to me. As a teen, feeling unpopular, I prayed to God asking for a boyfriend. After a while, a boy asked me out on a date. I knew then that God was *real*.

Once married, our family always went to church. It was an important part of our lives. When times are difficult, I pray, and I'm patient because God sometimes says, *No!* but he always has something else good in mind for me. He did not heal my husband's cancer, but when my husband passed away and I asked God, *What do I do for the rest of my life?* he presented me with ten years of volunteering for Habitat for Humanity, church mission trips, and other things I have loved.

*

The previous testimonies shared by church-goers reveals a segment of the worldview they adhere to. It is self-explanatory and there is no need for me to reiterate the beliefs here. However, it is clearly evident that faith can have a powerful impact upon lives both, through childhood, and as an adult. It is evident that having religious conviction helps people to endure much suffering in their personal lives as well as in their service to other human beings. Missionary work, in particular, demands an extreme amount of self-denial and sacrifice. Only by God's power can this be accomplished, and by God's protection in dangerous parts of the world. Others shared their vocations and have provided similar self-sacrifice. As the saying goes: Actions speak louder than words. They showed their faith by how they lived.

You will find all kinds of people on the religious spectrum when you walk through church doors. Some people in a Christian organization will claim to be Christians but they do nothing to help other people, living completely self-centered and selfish lives. Then you have the pluralist who has no clue as to who or what Christ is, who dedicates their life to serving others, especially serving the poor and oppressed, working for justice. The chaplain sister tried to figure this out—the apparent contradictions—but got nowhere in her thinking. God will judge, she thought, not I. Only God knows the truth of what is going on.

The chaplain thought all the people who answered her questionnaire really put a lot of emphasis on parental or grand-parental guidance. This appears to be central to their childhood. Brought to a church early in life for the majority, was significant in building their faith. All of the participants chosen for the study had exemplary character and the responses revealed that religion was an important factor in forming this character. For most of them, it gave them strength to help them through life's difficulties. If a participant was not exposed to church early on, they still had strong, parental role models and had within them a steady conscience that guided them through their positive life choices.

The chaplain thought, *what are we to make of this?* How can the mentally ill on psych units who are struggling psychologically and with physical survival issues, get help? After much prayer, the chaplain thought she'd create a curriculum, a new support group program titled *Spiritual Care on Psychiatric Units*, that she would distribute across the country's hospitals. This, she felt, would have the potential to awaken psychiatric patients' call to God, and by God. She set about creating this curriculum for spiritual support groups to be held on the psych units. She wrote up and compiled hope worksheets, and other materials about such issues as bullying or life choices. Fortunately, as a chaplain, she was allowed to do this even in secular facilities since she had a shoe in the door as an employed spiritual director. The groups would meet three times a week, perhaps just enough time to instill some inner strength and to inspire spiritual thoughts. The chaplain knew that once discharged from the hospital the patients would probably lack needed support for further spiritual exploration. She decided to pray about this for possible solutions. At any rate, the spiritual care groups meeting on psych units was a beginning. It would prove to the patients that there is a God who cares about them and is reaching out to them. And that they can begin a new, healthy life, moving forward in the recovery process.

The chaplain heard later on that some patients would take the initiative upon discharge to purchase Bibles themselves. Some found the courage to attend worship services at a local church. The healing for the patients was sometimes slow and arduous work, but many persisted. Social integration within the Christian community was tedious and slow, but the former patients found some support and, with time, some friends.

It's not always a happy ending, though. The chaplain knew that there are some psychiatric patients who find the challenges too daunting, losing hope. They give up entirely, succumbing to alcohol and illegal drug use, prostitution, and crime. There are some who struggle so much financially that they end up homeless and die on the street. And there are some church communities who just out-right reject the former patient who walks through their doors seeking welcome. Perhaps the former patient can't afford nice church clothes and isn't able to dress-up. So they don't fit in. There are many reasons a person might be rejected, including prejudice and discrimination. This is why pastors need to continue to preach about the compassion of Christ and how Christ's followers need to emulate him. This is why Sunday School classes should instruct young children and youth of all ages, to be kind and loving to other human beings, especially those who are different. For hearing these things is essential to healing our world. Hearing promotes doing. Good examples inspire others to do likewise. The many people with Christ-like character in churches provide examples for all to learn from. The chaplain thought, *let us pray for teachable hearts.*

Conclusion

As the chaplain sister continued her work amongst the poverty-stricken mentally ill, she recalled what Jesus had said to the rich Pharisees and rulers:

> "You are those who justify yourselves before men, but God knows your hearts; for what is exalted among men is an abomination in the sight of God . . . There was a rich man, who was clothed in purple and fine linen and who feasted sumptuously every day. And at his gate lay a poor man named Lazarus, full of sores, who desired to be fed with what fell from the rich man's table; moreover, the dogs came and licked his sores. The poor man died and was carried by the angels to Abraham's bosom. The rich man also died and was buried; and in Hades, being in torment, he lifted up his eyes, and saw Abraham far off and Lazarus in his bosom. And he called out, 'Father Abraham, have mercy upon me, and send Lazarus to dip the end of his finger in water and cool my tongue; for I am in anguish in this flame.' But Abraham said, 'Son, remember that you in your lifetime received your good things, and Lazarus in like manner bad things; but now he is comforted here, and you are in anguish. And besides all this, between us and you a great chasm has been fixed, in order that those who would pass from here to you may not be able, and none may cross from there to us.' And he said, 'Then I beg you, father, to send him to my father's house, for I have five brothers, so that he may warn them, lest they also come into this place of torment.' But Abraham said, 'They have Moses and the

prophets; let them hear them.' And he said, 'No, father Abraham; but if someone goes to them from the dead, they will repent.' He said to him, 'If they do not hear Moses and the prophets, neither will they be convinced if someone should rise from the dead.'" (Luke 16: 15, 19–31 ESV)

The above biblical text mentions the poor man's dietary deprivation as a result of being excluded and callous hearts. To widen the scope in a modern context, how has the barbed wire excluded others? Do the poor have decent housing and adequate clothing? What are the opportunities for an overall decent standard of living where dignity and survival are the concerns of families, local, state, or federal governments? Where general and psychiatric healthcare is accessible? And, then, how are people psychologically and spiritually nourished no matter the culture, gender, or abilities; where there is freedom of religious opinion and expression, and the freedom to assemble? Where all are welcome in educational systems and libraries; where all have a right to representation in a court of law, and a fair trial, and freedom from torture? And to be free of harassment and assault in one's own habitation?

There is much work to be done. No, an easy life is not the Christian way for we are called to carry one another's burdens, yes, to actually suffer, if need be, and so fulfil the law of Christ (Galatians 6:2 ESV). Social change is difficult and requires a lifetime of hard work and sacrifice. Disregarding others who are oppressed will not promote the many changes that need to be done. There are people who say: *I pulled myself up by my own bootstraps, I am a self-made man!* This is a great show of ignorance and an excuse to live a self-centered life. Reading books, news outlets, and socializing with diverse economic groups is the education for understanding the many accidents of history and life circumstances that play a part in human suffering and oppression. The marginalized, mentally ill population is on the outside of the mainstream for many reasons many of which are not self-inflicted. Stepping away from the many distractions we busy ourselves with and actually *listening to others* will allow for compassion to grow in our hearts. God calls all people to lend a hand. As long as there is a homeless man sleeping on the city's sidewalk during the night; as long as there is one hungry child, one victim of human trafficking or when war rages—God calls all of us to be instruments of mercy and peace.

In much of the chaplain's work she found the issue of *forgiveness* or *how to forgive*, something that is up front and center. With all the factors (biological, social, etc.) that promote mental health recovery, forgiveness is rarely mentioned in most psychiatric circles. First off, we need to be made right with our Creator; and for a believer, that is God. Knowing we have a sinful nature, corrupt from birth (or conception even), repentance is in order. At some point in our life, we feel the conviction of sin by the Holy Spirit. This convinces us we must be contrite of heart and tell God we're sorry. As we confess sins and feel forgiven, this frees us to a new life where we can breathe freer.

In order to be made right with God, we also acknowledge that some people have mistreated us (who may have done us great harm) and we must try to forgive them. Sometimes, it takes asking God to fill us with the forgiveness because we don't have the strength or power to do it ourselves. Praying for God's help is often needed. Mental health is greatly affected by the grudges we carry around, as well as the burdens of our own sins. Monitoring ourselves is helpful in this regard.

For centuries the mental health field has been dominated by secular ideas in the humanist realm of Western culture. Religious belief has been labeled psychopathic, a fantasy, disease, and disorder of the mind. Most physicians in the field of psychiatry have long held that the physical brain is broken in mental illness with no regard for the spiritual aspects of the mind or the concept of the soul. The brain and spirit can, and often does, operate in tandem. In this work, the author illustrated through stories and essays how vitally important religious belief is for the healthy functioning of individual human beings and society as a whole. A good quality of life depends on a relationship with the Creator and when a person turns their back on God this is the surest route to destruction.

God is patient with us. In a busy world, humans would benefit from taking some time out to reflect on our purpose in life. This isn't new, but it's often ignored, so bears repeating.

Bibliography

Murphy, Marcia A. "Having Tea," *Education/Advocacy*. Hope for Recovery. https://hopeforrecovery.com/having-tea-with-anne-hutchinson-justice-four-centuries-later/

———. *Reflections on the Meaning of Integrity: Recovery from Serious Mental Illness*. Eugene: Resource, 2021.

———. *Voices in the Rain: Meaning in Psychosis*. Eugene: Resource, 2018.

Pearce, Michelle J. "Religion Needs Seat." https://societyforpsychotherapy.org/why-religion-needs-a-seat-at-psychotherapys-table/

Universal Declaration of Human Rights. *30 Basic Human Rights List*. https://opseu.org/wp-content/uploads/2018/12/30_basic_human_rights_list_english.pdf

Wikipedia, *Ableism*. https://en.wikipedia.org/wiki/Ableism

Wikipedia, *Anne Hutchinson*. https://en.wikipedia.org/wiki/Anne_Hutchinson

Wikipedia, *Thomas Welde*. https://en.wikipedia.org/wiki/Thomas_Welde

www.ingramcontent.com/pod-product-compliance
Lightning Source LLC
Chambersburg PA
CBHW061249040426
42444CB00010B/2308